Illustrations by Belinda Willson

ISBN: 1 86476 235 7

Copyright © Axiom Publishing, 2003.
Unit 2, 1 Union Street, Stepney, South Australia, 5069.

This book is copyright. Apart from any fair dealing for the purpose of private study, research, criticism or review, as permitted under the Copyright Act, no part may be reproduced by any process without written permission.
Enquiries should be made to the publisher.
www.axiomdistributors.com.au

Printed in Malaysia

SHOPPING LIST

Count the fruit and vegetables and write the numbers on the shopping list. The first one is done for you.

SEASONS

Draw a line from the seasons to the clothes

Summer Winter

WHAT IS IT?

Unjumble the word to find out what these are. Here is a clue, birds have them.

R E A F H T E S   _ _ _ _ _ _ _ _

SUMS AND COLOURING

Do the sums then colour the drawing using the code.

6 = green   4 = red   7 = brown
3 = blue   5 = orange   8 = yellow

WHERE DO THEY LIVE?

Draw a line from the people to their homes.

Child

Eskimo

Indian

Draw where you live.

SPELLING

Complete the words using the clues to help you.

h, or gh

ni _ _ t

li _ _ tning

t _ under

ostric _

mot _

_ orse

l, or ll

she _ _

sea _

turt _ e

caterp _ _ a r

butterf _ y

mi _ _ ipede

n, m or mm

hu _ _ ing bird

e _ u

_ o _ key

rai _ bow

s _ ail

bu _ ble bees

o, or oo

m _ _ n

z _ _

d _ lphin

c _ w

st _ rm

bab _ _ n

COLOURING

W Winter WINTER

Draw 4 more snow flakes

Snowman

COUNTING SKILLS

How many monkeys can you count?

As number _   As word _ _ _ _

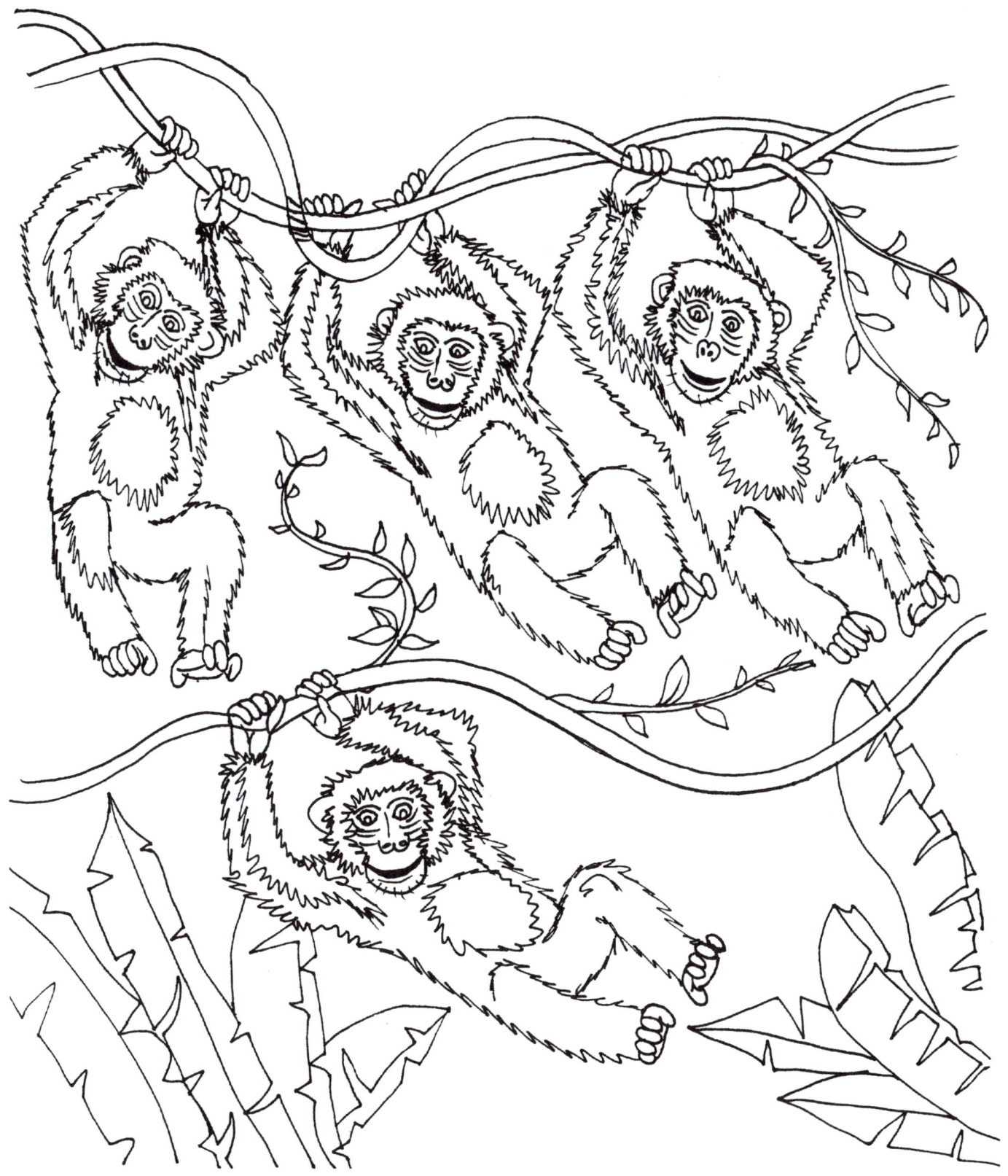

MOUNTAINS

Look at this picture and draw a line from the word to the part of the picture it describes.

clouds

sky

river

pine trees

snow

rocks

mountains

birds

DOT TO DOT

Connect the dots to see what a Yak looks like.

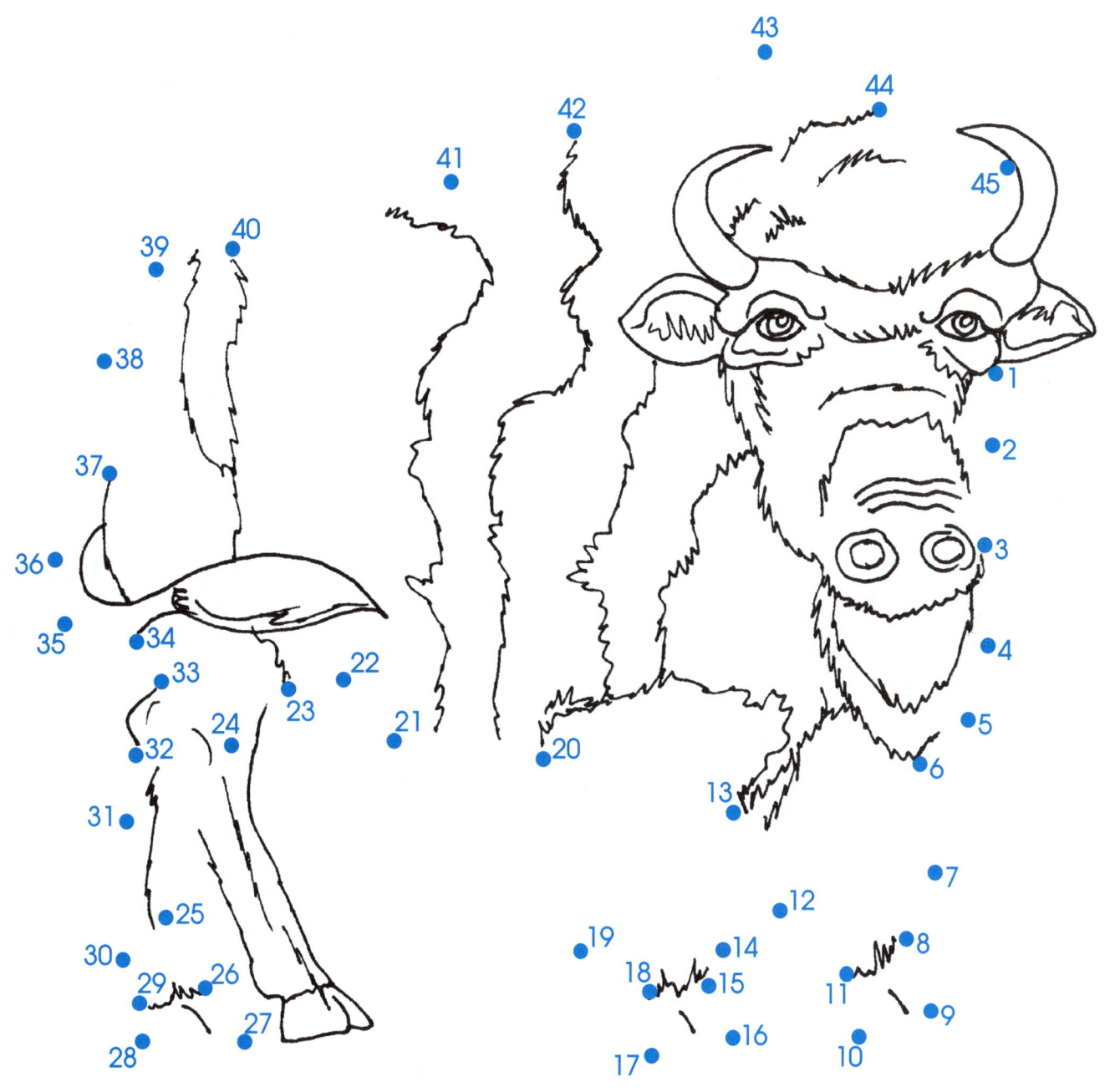

SEASONS

Unjumble the words to find out what season this is. Write the words below. Colour the leaves 2 red, 2 yellow, 2 orange.

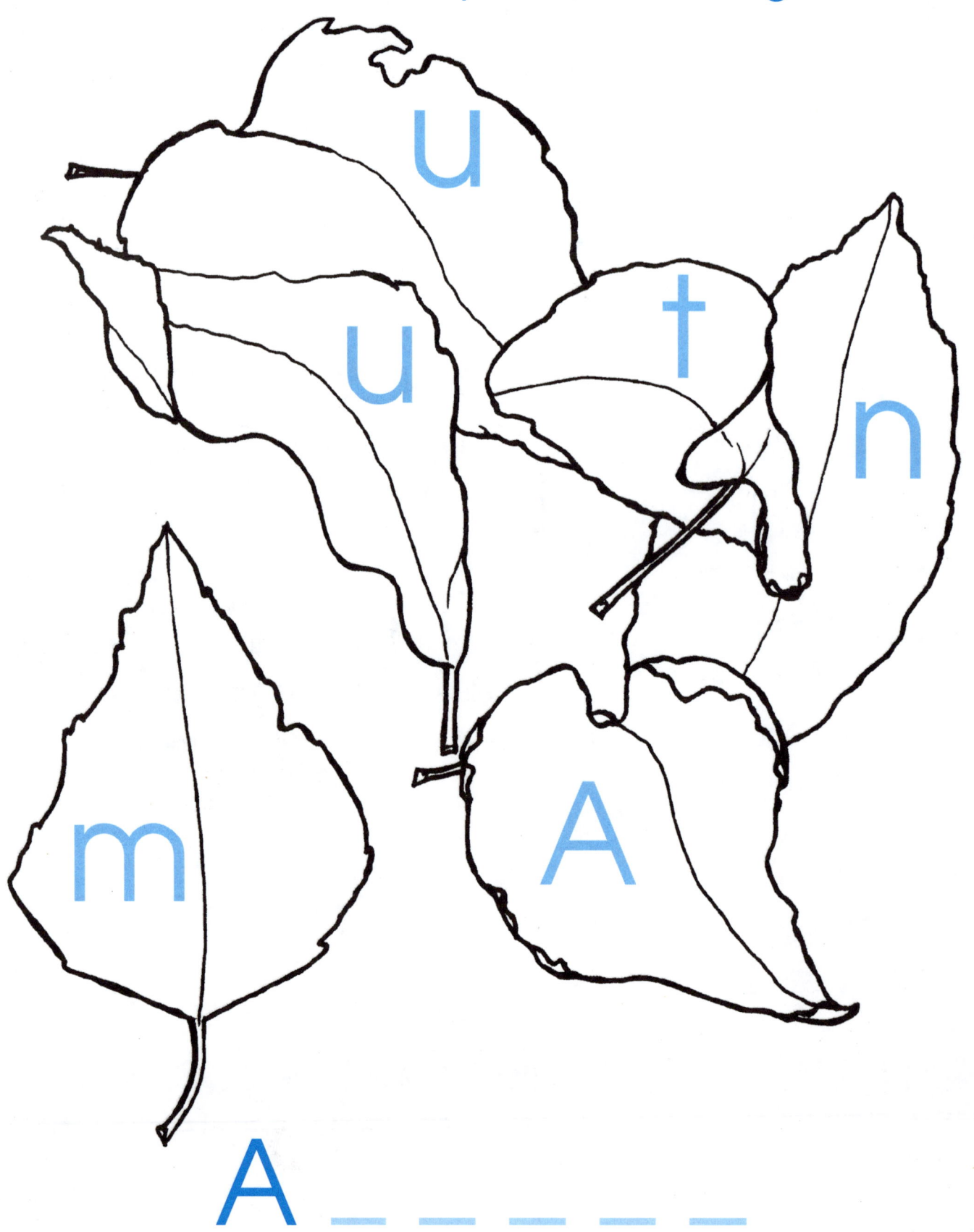

A _ _ _ _ _

WORD SKILLS

L
Circle words that begin with the letter L.

lioness   paws   liver   lost

lame   lama   lizard   lovely   brown

horse   camel   mane   tail

COLOURING

Colour objects that protect you from the sun, red.
* Something to sit on and dry yourself with green.
* Something to carry on your shoulder and put things in, blue.
* What you swim in yellow.
* Bucket & spade, pink.
* Something to play catch with, red, blue, orange.

LETTER SKILLS

A a   Antarctica

Antarctica

A _____

DRAWING

Look at the tags in each pot to find how many flowers to draw.
Copy the pictures on the pots.

NUMBER SKILLS

How many owls can you count? Write your answer in the circle.

DOT TO DOT

Join the dots and unscramble the words to find who this is.

HWLAE _ _ _ _ _

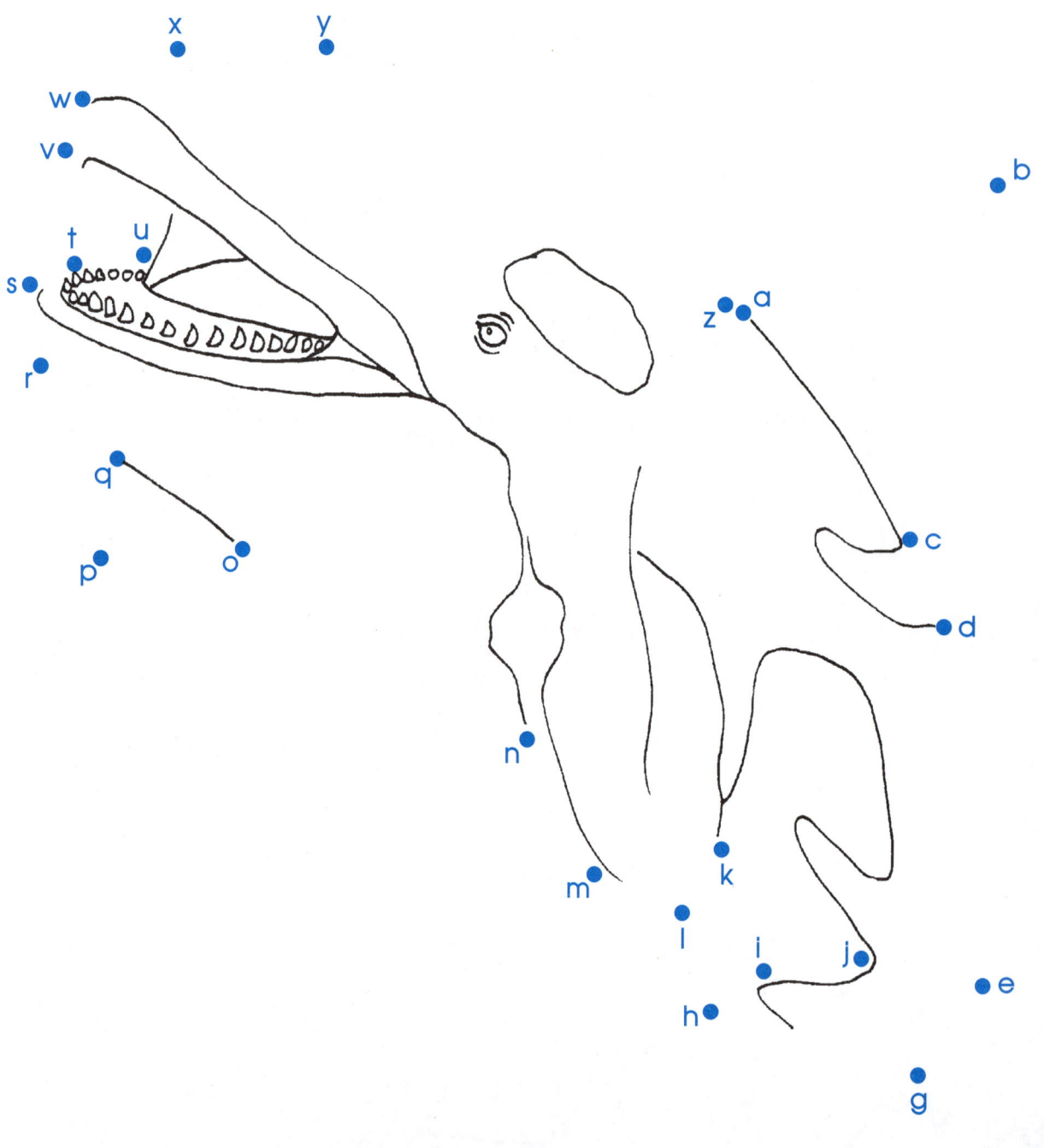

COLOURING AND DRAWING

Colour the photos of the flowers and trees.

Draw a photo of your favourite place or things.

WORD SKILLS

Circle words about water and how it is useful. Colour the water in the glass the colour of your favourite drink.

COLOURING

What is wrong with this picture? Colour the 5 objects that do not belong.

DRAW LINES

Draw a line from the food to where it comes from.

bee

bread

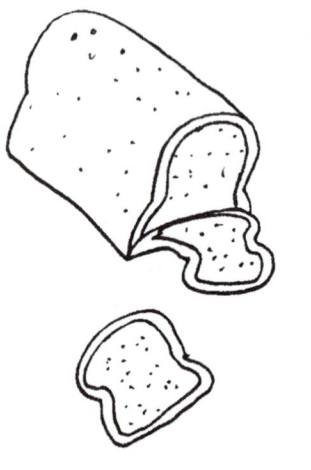

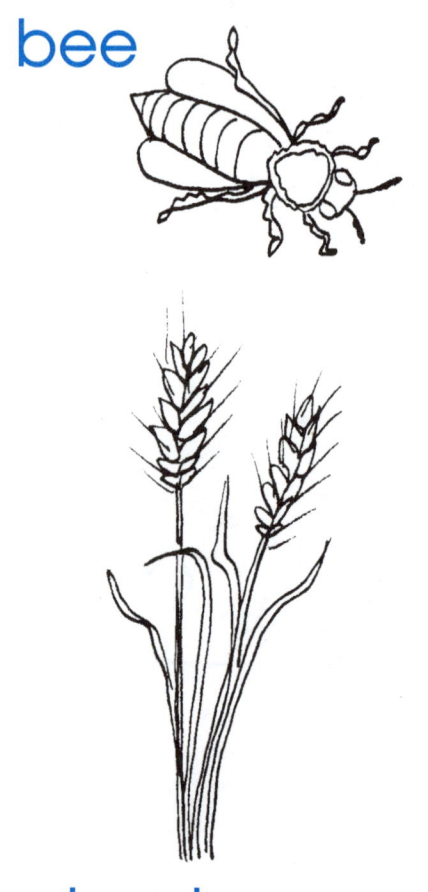

honey

wheat

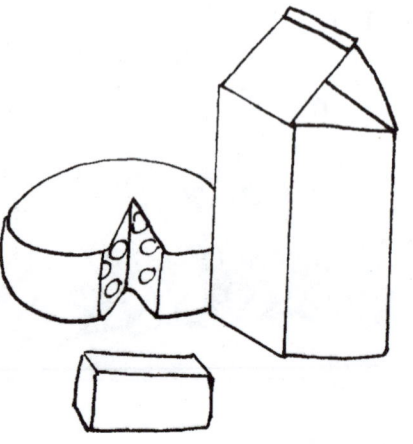

milk, cheese, butter

DOT TO DOT

Follow the numbers from 1 to 28 and connect the dots to find out who this is.

FIND THE PATH

Help the honey bee find his way to the flower to collect pollen.

WORD SKILLS

The sloth is a slow creature. It likes to hang upside down from branches. Sloths sleep a lot and carry their babies on their tummies.

branches   slow   brown   ran   bobbies
fast   up   tall   sloth   sleep   carry
blue   awake   very   down

Circle the words that appear in the sentences above

OBSERVATION
What do these things have in common?

WORD SKILLS

Use the words inside the tree to complete the sentences.

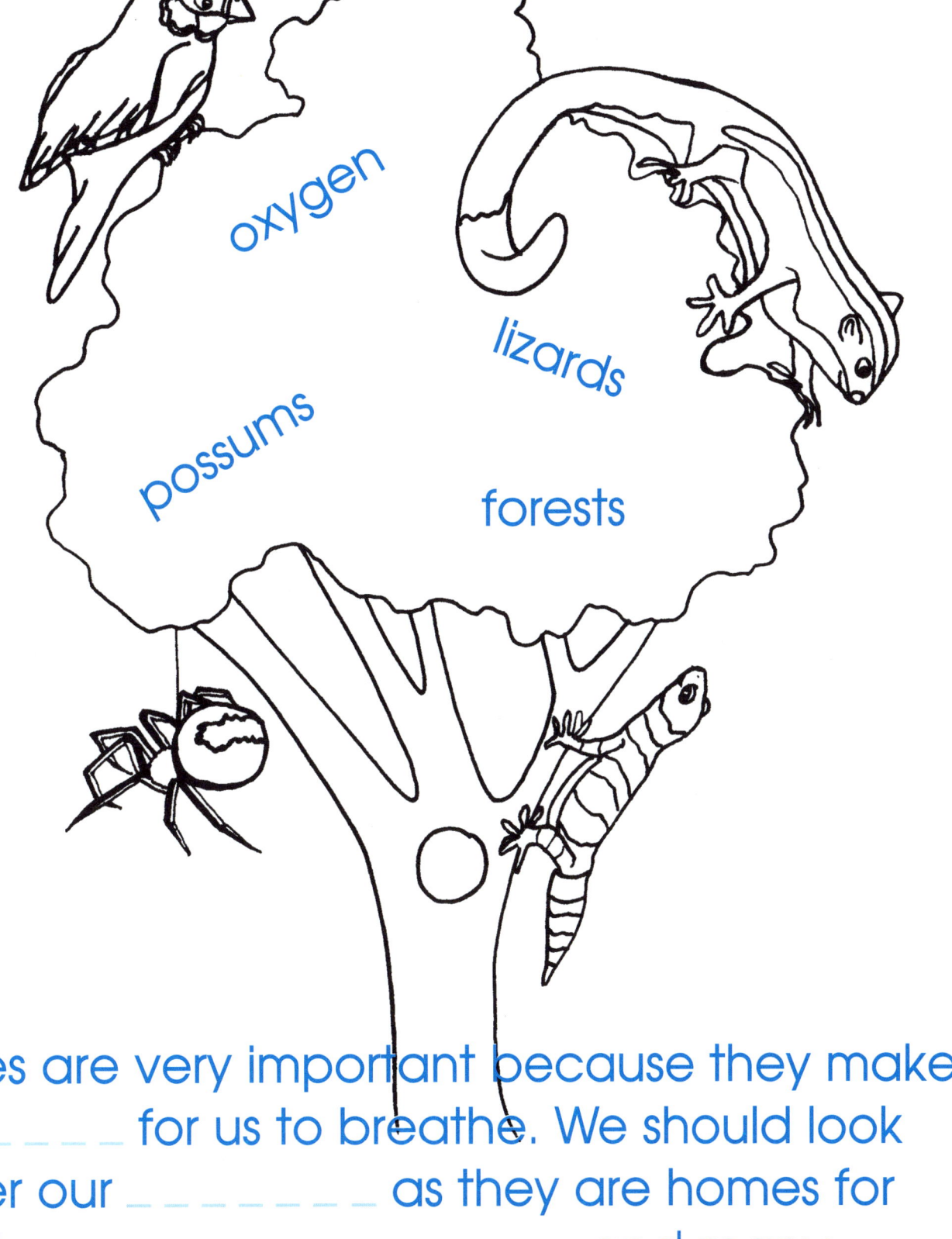

oxygen, lizards, possums, forests

Trees are very important because they make _____ for us to breathe. We should look after our _____ as they are homes for birds, _____, _____ and many creatures.

COLOURING

W w whale
WHALE

Whale

W____

WORD SKILLS

Ww wolf
WOLF

Right or Left

Which wolf is on the left and which is on the right? Draw a line from each wolf to the correct word.

WHO IS THIS?

Connect the dots by following the words in alphabetical order.

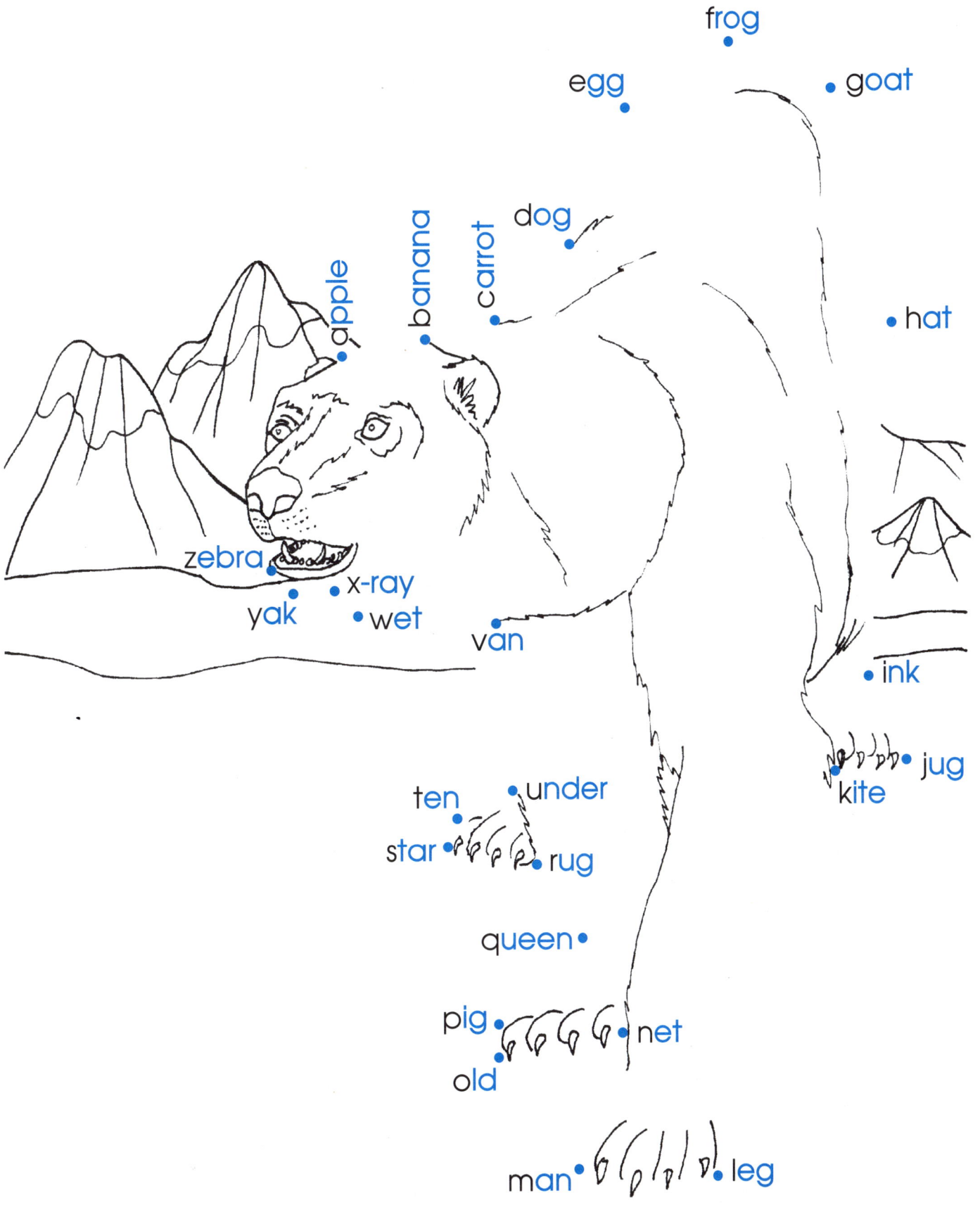

NUMBER SKILLS

Write the answer to each question in the circle.

How many swans are there? ◯

Baby swans are called singnets, how many are there? ◯

How many adults are there? ◯

Draw 3 more swans. How many are there now? ◯